the "Green" Gardener

the "Green" Gardener

Working *With* Nature, Not Against It

Brenda Little

SILVERLEAF
PRESS

Silverleaf Press Books are available exclusively
through Independent Publishers Group.

For details write or telephone
Independent Publishers Group, 814 North Franklin St.
Chicago, IL 60610, (312) 337-0747

Silverleaf Press
8160 South Highland Drive
Sandy, Utah 84093

ISBN-10: 1-933317-80-9
ISBN-13: 978-1-933317-80-9

3689 2080 12/07

Contents

INTRODUCTION 9

1. IMPROVING THE SOIL 13
Growing Green • Improving the Soil • Mushroom
Compost •Peat Moss •Compost • Compost Without
a Heap • Composting in Small Spaces •Weeds Can Be
Useful

2. CREATING GREEN GARDENS . . 41
No-Dig Gardening • Companion
Planting

3. FERTILIZING THE GARDEN. . 49
Animal Manures • Man Manure • Ocean
Manure • Other Organic Fertilizers

4. MULCH. 61
Proceeds from Processing • Lucerne Hay • Leaf Mulch •
Lawn Clippings • Weeds • Newspaper • Sawdust • Pine
Needles • Bark Mulch • Inorganic Mulch

5. SAVING WATER. 77
Saving the Bath Water • Good Watering Techniques •
Watering Established Trees • Choose Drought-Tolerant
Plants • Planting for Success with Minimum Water

6. WILDLIFE IN THE GARDEN. 93
Birds • Other Visitors

7. CONTROLLING PESTS AND DISEASES. 101
Attracting the Right Insects • Sprays for Pest and
Diseases • Recipes • Trap that Pest • Change Your Ways

"The glory of gardening: hands in the dirt, head in the sun, heart with nature. To nurture a garden is to feed not just on the body, but the soul."

....

~Alfred Austin

Introduction

Over the years, gardening has become more and more popular. There are now many of us who no longer want to indulge in expensive ways of entertaining ourselves in our spare time and who have moved into a more thoughtful, stay-at-home mode. We prefer to contemplate the problems of the world from the safe distance of our personal havens.

And certainly there are problems all around us. On our televisions and in our newspapers we see the evidence of the world dying. The destruction of the rainforests, the gradual extinction of endangered species of flora and fauna, massive oil spills creating havoc in our oceans, soil salination ruining our lands; these are just some of our modern horrors. They are huge, and hugely depressing, problems about which we as individuals can do little on a global scale. But we can act locally, in our own backyards: we can go green in the garden.

The simple act of gardening and growing things is a creative exercise that is enriching to the spirit. Green gardening is doubly rewarding because it is not just plants that flourish under your attention, but the whole ecosystem of your backyard.

Green gardening means using organic methods of growing plants, fertilizing the soil, and controlling insect pests. Green methods allow earthworms and tiny soil organisms to multiply and help plants grow more strongly. Birds and lizards can visit the garden without the threat of being poisoned by

pesticide residues. The vegetables and fruit we grow with green methods are naturally wholesome. The world may be in disarray, but at least on our side of the picket fence nature won't be taking a beating.

If you don't have space for a garden, you can still help save the earth through green gardening practices: join one of the neighborhood groups working to regenerate a local piece of wilderness; garden on a vacant lot (there are permaculture groups helping people to garden on abandoned land in inner-city areas as well as in country areas); become a volunteering parent in one of your school's greening programs; become a gardening friend for historic houses and gardens; or go tree-planting with local organizations.

Being a green gardener requires some changes to what have become accepted methods, but it doesn't have to be a problem. Backsliders can repent and start afresh. With practice you will find it an enjoyable and rewarding way of gardening. It keeps you healthy (no nasty sprays to breathe or handle), keeps your plants healthy, keeps you interested, and makes your garden an expression of your own ideals and concern for the environment.

This book will help you achieve the aims of the green gardener. It tells how to create the right conditions for a healthy garden, explains how to minimize problems with pests and diseases, and gives environmentally friendly solutions for problems that do arise. Following the advice here, coupled with the experience you have of your own piece of the environment, you will be able to create a truly safe haven in your garden.

"A garden requires patient labor and attention. Plants do not grow merely to satisfy ambitions or to fulfill good intentions. They thrive because someone expended effort on them."

....

~Liberty Hyde Bailey

Chapter 1

Improving the Soil

Growing Green

Being a green gardener means using gardening methods with minimum toxicity for humans, mammals, and such beneficial garden residents and visitors as birds, reptiles, spiders, and insects. It also means disrupting the environment beyond the garden as little as possible, through, for example, the seepage of chemicals; using nonrenewable resources only when absolutely essential and making maximum use of recycling and waste minimization.

Most gardeners considering a greener approach are looking for alternatives to poisons in

Testing soil

1. To test for the degree of acidity, collect samples without touching them with your hands.
2. Add the soil carefully to a test tube containing an indicator solution. Shake.
3. Compare the color of the shaken solution, after it has settled with the chart supplied with the kit.

You can also test soil acidity with litmus paper, available at most drugstores.

treating pest and disease problems. But before we get to cures, let's look first at prevention. Most pests and diseases attack unhealthy plants. (Though this isn't always the case—snails and slugs love strong healthy growth and aphids are always found where young growth is lushest.) Growing healthy plants is the first step in reducing problems with pests and disease and so reducing your reliance on toxic solutions.

The golden rule in growing healthy plants is to provide the right conditions. Choose plant material that suits your climate, find a position that meets its sunlight requirements and, most importantly, look to your soil.

Ten Commandments for the Green Gardener

1. Have a compost heap and learn to compost efficiently.
2. Use non-toxic methods of controlling pests and diseases when possible.
3. Mulch garden beds every three or four months.
4. Make efficient use of water.
5. Grow plants that do not need frequent spraying to keep them healthy.
6. Always read the label on containers of garden sprays carefully before purchase. This will help you avoid the more toxic sprays.
7. Follow the directions, using the amounts recommended.
8. Spray in the cool of a calm day for safe and effective results.
9. Keep up garden "housekeeping" by cleaning up rubbish that could harbor dangerous spiders, or provide a watery home for mosquito larvae.
10. Love your garden and enjoy the wholesome and creative activity of gardening and beautifying your own patch of the planet Earth.

Improving the Soil

Good soil looks crumbly, is rich in earthworms and organic matter, and does not dry out too fast or cake. It does not go into a thick glue when wet and does not stay waterlogged for long periods after rain.

So what sort of soil do you have in your garden? Scrape up a handful of damp soil and squeeze it in your hand. If it retains its shape, it is clay. If it takes some shape but remains crumbly, it is loam, and if it simply falls away, it is sandy.

Clay soils are rich in nutrients, but if too heavy and sticky, plants can't grow well. Loam soils are excellent: easy to dig and with good water-holding ability. Sandy soils are poor, with little or no water-holding capacity. Water and nutrients are leached quickly so that sandy soils need frequent watering and feeding with small amounts of fertilizer.

It doesn't matter how poor your soil is, you can improve it by adding as much humus as possible to the top 4–6 inches (10–15cm) of soil. Good sources of humus include spent mushroom compost, peat moss and its substitutes, and compost. Additions of humus need to be made three or four times a year.

Preparing your Dirt

1. Dig over the beds with a hoe.

2. Water and fork it over.

3. Sprinkle lime, then add humus.

4. Dig through thoroughly and water.

PEAT MOSS

Lime Lights

❦ Lime is a useful aid for the green gardener, as long as care is taken not to use it around acid-soil-loving plants, such as azaleas and camellias.

❦ If your garden is troubled by fungal diseases that stay in the soil and re-infect plants year after year, try liming the bed at the rate of 1 cup per square meter. Fungus thrives in acid soils, so making the soil more alkaline will reduce the ability of the fungal spores to survive. Roses are prone to fungal diseases in humid coastal climates and giving roses a dressing of lime (2½ teaspoons per square foot/a half cup per square meter in light soils, 1½ tablespoons per square foot/1 cup per square meter in heavy clay soils) should help reduce fungal attack. The foliage of roses and apple trees can also be sprayed with lime mixed with water to reduce the pH of the leaves. Most winter sprays, such as lime sulfur and Bordeaux, contain some sort of lime wash.

❦ If you have a tree or other plants in the garden that are affected by herbicide or other poisonous substances, lime the soil and water in well to inactivate the poison. A dressing of lime, plus a really good soaking will help counteract the damage, which is most likely to happen if the weather is dry.

❦ Lime will also protect clivias from snails. Clivias are very prone to being damaged by snails that live under the cool damp leaves and feed on the flowers at night. Protect the blooms by dusting the plants with lime. The easiest way to do this is to first hose the clumps well, making sure to wet under the leaves. Then dip a piece of hairy material, such as burlap, towel material, or wool into the lime so that it is well-coated with the dust. Push the cloth into the clump and shake it vigorously. The fine lime dust will fly up and cling to the wet foliage, where it will effectively control the snails and save your flowers. Of course, don't use this treatment around any plants that prefer acid conditions.

❧ To sweeten compost bins made smelly by too much moisture or an imbalance of citrus skins, scatter a handful of lime over the heap and water it in lightly. Leave the cover off the bin for a day or two to help it dry out. A handful of lime added to the heap occasionally will speed up the compost process, especially if it contains hard-to-compost ingredients such as pine needles.

❧ Blossom end rot of tomatoes is caused by a deficiency of calcium in the soil. The soil should be limed or have superphosphate added before planting. Plants should also be watered regularly. Drainage or water-holding capacity of the soil may also need improving. Water with a surfactant and dig in plenty of humus.

❧ Oxalis grows in acid soils and will not grow as vigorously if you reduce the acidity in areas that are infested with oxalis.

❧ Lime will also pink your hydrangeas. Scatter a dressing of lime around plants in spring to make the soil more alkaline and so produce pink flowers.pass so that by the time the acid-loving tomatoes have their turn, the soil will be perfect for them.

Clay soils need to be dug and treated with gypsum to develop a more crumbly soil structure. Dig humus into each planting hole, mixing it thoroughly with the existing soil. Mulch the surface of the soil regularly. Try to practice no-dig gardening—don't dig down into the clay, but keep building up above it with added compost and mulch. Raised beds make this easier. Sandy soils need just as much humus as clay soils. When planting, line the planting hole with two or three sheets of newspaper, then fill the hole with compost and soil mixed well together. Add water crystals that absorb water so that there is a reservoir of moisture that doesn't soak away. The newspaper will compost down, but will slow the leaching of water and fertilizer until plants can get their roots established.

Newspaper can also be shredded and partly mixed into the surface of sandy soils where it will retain moisture, attract earthworms (which don't generally like sandy soils), and compost down well to enrich the soil. Recycling newspaper in this way is an inexpensive method of improving sandy soils.

Good soil not only requires a good texture through the addition of plenty of organic matter, but also good drainage. You can tell if your drainage is satisfactory by filling a hole you have dug for a tree or shrub with water. If the water drains away instantly, you will have a problem retaining enough moisture to grow a wide variety of plant material and need to add humus in as large a quantity as you can manage.

If the water drains away within a few minutes, drainage is satisfactory. But if the water takes several hours to drain away, or if you dig a hole and find the following day that water has seeped into it, you have a drainage problem. The only way to really fix such a problem

Soil Profile

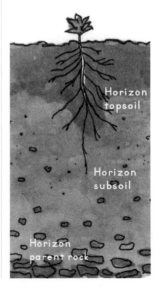

Horizon topsoil

Horizon subsoil

Horizon parent rock

is by installing agricultural pipes to carry the surplus water away. Alternately, think of the area as a natural bog and grow swamp-loving plants.

Mushroom Compost

Spent mushroom compost is mostly a mixture of composted manure, straw, and peat moss—all good, organic ingredients—and is a good way of adding humus and bulk to the soil. Gardeners who live in an area where there are commercial mushroom farms will find spent mushroom compost available by the truckload. It is also available in bags in nurseries and garden supply centers.

Mushroom compost is an especially good addition to sandy soils as it is dense and doesn't leach down through the soil too rapidly. It also improves the water-holding capacity and drainage of heavy soils. Mix it with potting mix to give more humus to the mixture if growing shrubs in containers for the long-term.

The pH of spent mushroom compost may be variable. Before using large amounts, it is advisable to check the pH using a home garden soil testing kit. This is particularly

important if you are planting acid-loving plants
such as camellias and azaleas, which need a slightly
acid soil to grow well. Mushroom compost is
generally alkaline, with a high pH.

If you do buy a batch of spent mushroom
compost with a high pH, the pH can be lowered
by sprinkling the heap with sulfur (flowers of
sulfur). The following rates are recommended:
2½–4½ tablespoons per square yard (30–60
grams per square meter) for sandy soils,
4½–7 tablespoons per square yard (60–90
grams per square meter) for loam, and 7–7½
tablespoons per square yard (90–100 grams
per square meter) for clay. Water the heap
lightly; fork over to distribute the sulfur
evenly; then gently water again. Leave
the heap for a few days and re-test before
using. The addition of as much leaf
mulch as possible will also increase the
acidity and help lower the pH.

Peat Moss

This is a fairly expensive way to add humus to the garden but

Different Types of Compost Bins

Gedye Bin

The Gedye compost bin is easy for suburban gardeners. This is a fluted bin that must be stationed on bare soil. The open bottom allows the worms to get into the bin. When the compost is ready, the bin is removed leaving a compost "cake."

Traditional Bin

Layering the compost bin as shown here is a traditional way of making compost and is designed to increase the rate of decay.

lime
grass cuttings
horse manure (or straw)
lime
leaves
horse manure
grass cuttings
horse manure

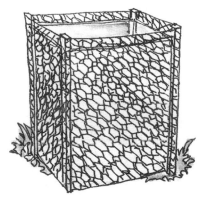

Wire Mesh Bins

Wire mesh bins are inexpensive, but the compost may be slow to generate heat and to decompose.

Composting Bays

Build three bays as shown. The first for storing and collecting organic matter, the second for the breakdown stage, and the third for compost ready to use. Make sure there are air spaces between the boards.

it is an excellent material and is often used in potting mix for camellias and azaleas, which appreciate the resulting acid soil. Unfortunately peat moss is dug from peat bogs and this is doing great damage to the environment of areas where peat is being mined commercially, such as in Ireland and Germany.

Environmentally conscious gardeners will not want to use large quantities of peat moss. Fortunately, more sustainable alternatives are available, generally made from coconut husks, a waste product of coconut processing. The husk product can be used successfully as a replacement for peat in potting mixes and as a soil additive in gardens.

Coco-peat and other similar brands are completely organic and are recommended to the green gardener.

Compost

A compost heap is absolutely essential for all green gardeners as it not only takes garden and kitchen waste out of our overwhelmed waste stream, but also provides

Compost Tumblers

A compost tumbler is a drum mounted on a strong frame with an axle that allows the drum to be revolved. The tumbler is revolved for a few minutes each day and this aerates and speeds up the compost so that it can be ready to use two weeks after the drum has been filled. It is important to keep a well-balanced mixture of ingredients in your tumbler. Too many grass clippings or citrus skins will result in an unbalanced compost.

Compost tumblers can be bought or the handy person can make one with a good, clean drum (which has not contained toxic materials), a length of water pipe for an axle, and a strong frame.

Warning:

Never feed your worms dairy or meat products. And, before you put food in the bin, chop it into tiny pieces to speed decomposition.

valuable humus for the soil.

A lot of mystique is built up around composting, but it is basically very simple and easy to do.

There are many different ways of containing your compost, from a simple heap on the ground to timber or fiberglass bins. Use whichever method suits your space: the ideal of three matching timber slat bins takes up space many gardeners don't have. A heap on the ground with four boards or a row of bricks to contain it is the cheapest and easiest but does not appeal to tidy-minded gardeners.

Try this simple method, which is basically an open-ended basket. Drive three or four stakes into the ground in an out-of-the-way part of the garden. Wrap them with chicken wire or plastic mesh.

Put in your household peelings, eggshells, tea leaves, coffee grounds, vacuum cleaner dust, hair clippings (no food scraps). Add lawn clippings, fallen leaves, non-seeding annual weeds, spent plants, prunings, seaweed, sawdust, shredded paper—anything old and organic.

Cover the heap with a piece of heavy-duty plastic so that it doesn't get too wet in rain. The compost needs to be moist but not wet. Add a spadeful of soil or manure or compost accelerator when you make an addition to the heap.

If the compost heap is smelly, it is either too wet, in

Worms

Vermiculture is the technique of using worms to break down waste material. Some varieties of worms can survive temperatures up to 77°F (25°C) degrees but will die if the weather turns very cold or if the soil is excessively acidic. One worm can turn out its own weight in castings in one day. These castings are richer in minerals than the material ingested by the worm. Worms can break up hard soil and burrow to a depth of 7 feet (2m).

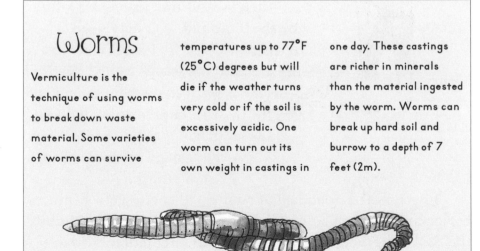

which case leave the cover off for a few days to allow moisture to evaporate, or food scraps are decomposing, or the balance of ingredients has gone off, perhaps with too many citrus skins. In those last cases, sprinkle a cup of lime over the surface, moisten it, and cover with a layer of soil.

Try to keep the ingredients fairly balanced. For instance, if you have huge amounts of lawn clippings, it is a good idea to start a separate heap where the over-supply can be piled up, mixed with manure and soil, and covered.

When the autumn leaves are falling by the thousand, you may need to make an extra basket where surplus leaves can be piled with some manure and soil to compost down without throwing the quantities in your main compost heap out of whack.

To generate a good heat, you need to aerate your heap by forking it through once or twice a week. But you will find the basket method allows for lots of air circulation. Add a

What Not to Compost

Almost anything can be composted, but there are exceptions:

🌸 **Meat and Meat Products**
These will not only cause your heap to smell, but will attract all kinds of pests, including rodents.

🌸 **Pet Litter**
Used kitty litter or dog and cat feces are not good additions to your heap. Both can carry disease.

🌸 **Barbecue Ashes**
Wood ashes from fireplaces can be valuable compost materials, but coal ashes from charcoal barbecues contain sulfur oxides and other compounds toxic to the soil.

🌸 **Diseased Garden Plants or Prunings**
Most home compost heaps don't generate the kind of heat needed to kill off the bacterium, virus, or fungus that caused the disease.

🌸 **Weed Seeds, Bulbs, or Tubers**
Again home compost heaps just aren't explosive enough to destroy seeds and bulbs, and the last thing you want is an increased weed problem. Get your own back on noxious weeds by putting them in a galvanized steel trash bin, covering with boiling water, mashing them a bit, and when they're cool, filling the bin with water. Put on the lid and leave the bin in a sunny place for a few months. Dilute the resulting liquid and use as a fertilizer.

🌸 **Magazines**
Though shredded newspapers do well in a compost heap, glossy magazines aren't a good idea. The inks used may contain toxins.

Weeds

Weeds can be put to use in the green garden. Most (except those with ripe seed heads or bulbous roots, such as oxalis) can be used safely in the compost heap or as mulch. Pull or slash weeds frequently to prevent them from setting seed. Seeds will be damaged in a compost heap only if you can manage the heating process effectively. Most home compost heaps don't really get hot enough to destroy all weed seeds; hence the number of avocados, tomatoes, and pumpkins that volunteer in compost.

If you don't have time to weed out whole plants, slash or pull off flowers and any young seed heads frequently this won't get rid of the weeds but will prevent them from seeding and spreading. That old saying: "One year's seeding means seven year's weeding" is not just an old gardener's tale. It's true.

Red Champion

Poppy

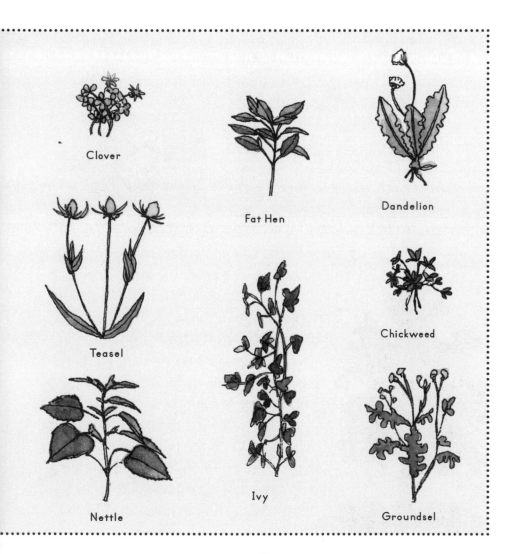

Clover

Fat Hen

Dandelion

Teasel

Chickweed

Nettle

Ivy

Groundsel

compost accelerator—either a commercial one or an herbal one that can be composed of comfrey nettles, dandelion, chamomile, and yarrow. If these herbs don't feature in the garden, try a chamomile tea bag. Pour 1 quart (1 liter) of boiling water over a chamomile teabag, allow to cool, then water over heap.

Earthworms will colonize your heap naturally, but if you want more, worm farms (sold in plastic, take-away food containers) are available from many nurseries or you can order them from worm farms advertised in gardening magazines. Put your worms down into the cooler, partly composted part of the heap. They will be burned in the heat further up.

Your compost will be ready when it becomes dark, crumbly soil. You can start mining it from the bottom of the heap while allowing the heap to continue to compost. Or, if the process is taking longer, close off the full bin and allow it to completely break down before using, while starting to fill a new bin.

Use compost as mulch over the soil surface or dig it into the top 5–6 inches (12–15cm) of soil before planting vegetables. In a no-dig garden, use compost in the planting holes in the mulch. For tree or shrub planting, mix compost well through existing soil in the planting hole. If growing plants in containers, use compost or half compost and potting mix or one-third each rotted manure, potting mix, and compost for a good, organic potting soil.

Compost Without a Heap

If you are making a new garden bed, you can put compost materials straight into the bed. Dig a trench along the length of the bed 5–7 inches (12–18cm) deep.

Empty your compost bucket into the trench and push in a light covering of soil, gradually moving along the trench as it fills. Fill to a level at least 5 inches (12cm) higher than the original soil level as compost reduces by one-third. Plant the filled section of the trench with seeds of quick-growing

annuals such as lupins, which have nitrogen-fixing roots.

By the time they are spent and ready to turn into the soil, your bed will be full of well-composted, enriched soil and ready for more permanent plantings.

Composting in Small Spaces

It's possible to have your own compost even if you garden on

a balcony, patio, or courtyard. Household scraps, leaves, weeds, spent plants, and flowers can be put into a container, such as a heavy-duty plastic bag or garbage bin. Make a few holes in the sides to help air circulation and keep the compost covered.

Even better are vermicomposters. You simply add earthworms and compostable material and remove the valuable vermicompost from a drawer in the bottom of the device. It is important to keep a good balance of materials in a small balcony composter. For instance, too many orange skins will make the compost very acid (and very smelly). Add fruit and vegetable peelings, dust from the vacuum bag, fallen leaves

and debris that can be swept up (often good compostable material can be found in the gutters or out on the nature strip), crushed eggshells, tea leaves, coffee grounds, and nut shells. Add a handful of fertilizer or animal manure, plus a dusting of lime (or dolomite if you grow azaleas and camellias), and a regular spade of soil. If you don't have access to soil, use potting mix and a container of worms, bought from the local nursery or worm farm.

Put the worms into the compost but don't let them come into contact with lime or fertilizer, which will burn them. Give them a bed of rotted leaves, a slice of bread, and a handful of bran and cover them with some lettuce leaves to get them started. Make sure they're cool and damp.

Earthworms will eat anything that was once living, but though adding bread, bran, or flour gives a start to newly added worms, it's not a good idea to make adding food scraps to a balcony composter a habit. Food scraps could attract undesirables such as ants, cockroaches, or even the dreaded rats. If you do have an active worm population, you can experiment with adding a variety of organic materials to feed your worms. They will quickly move into anything they like and have big appetites. The vegetable peels from one or two people won't be enough food for an active population, so remember to add extras like shredded newspapers and manure.

Once your container is full, start a second one. Remove some of the worm population with a spadeful of humus from the first bin, and use it to start off the second. You will be able to start using the compost as soon as it resembles soil. Use it in pots and containers on the balcony or spread it on any garden soil available as a mulch or dug lightly into the top 4–6 inches (10–15cm).

Weeds Can Be Useful

Some weeds, such as nettles, dandelions, and comfrey (an herb that grows like a weed) are great compost

Nettle

activators and make good green manure so can be very useful to the green gardener.

Stinging nettles are high in nitrogen and contain iron; dandelions have calcium; and comfrey leaves contain calcium, phosphorus, and potassium, so have plenty of goodness to contribute to the nutrient value of compost or green manure.

To make green manure from weeds, half fill a bucket or drum with weeds, such as stinging nettles, dandelions, and chickweed, and mash them up a bit and cover it all with boiling water. When cool, fill the container with water, cover, and leave for two or three weeks. Strain the liquid off and use it as needed. The residue left when the liquid has been strained off can go into the compost bin.

Comfrey

"Gardening is about enjoying the
smell of things growing in the soil,
getting dirty without feeling guilty, and
generally taking the time to soak up a
little peace and serenity."

....

~Lindley Karstens

Chapter 2

Creating Green Gardens

No-Dig Gardening

The no-dig garden is a great labor saver. It is achieved by building up a mulch—for example, of overlapped newspaper, spoiled alfalfa hay, and manure—over the surface of the soil.

This means you neither dig to prepare for planting, nor dig to remove weeds. No-dig is an excellent method for growing vegetables. To plant, make holes in the mulch, put in a spadeful of compost or potting mix and plant two or three vegetable

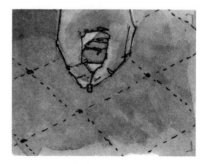

seeds in each hole. Water and wait. The seeds will germinate and grow, the roots spreading out into the mulch, which gradually breaks down.

When the next season comes around, the mulch has become a layer of good soil, which is topped up with the same layer cake of newspaper, hay, and manure. Doing this twice a year in spring and autumn when you make new plantings gradually builds up a bed of good, well-composted soil.

No-dig encourages earthworms to do the digging as they feed on the mulch, drawing it down into the topsoil, aerating and fertilizing as they move through it.

You can change to no-dig gardening in an established garden by mulching beds heavily 3–4 inches (8–10cm) deep. Do not let the mulch build up against the stems of established plants as it may cause rotting.

Regular mulching around a garden that is mainly shrubs and perennials will mean you never have to dig. Most plants will grow better if the gardener

making leaf mold Compost

1. If you are a good leaf scavenger, you will have a continual supply of leaves coming in. The easiest way to deal with them is to pile them in a shady spot and water them down.

2. Now sprinkle a light layer of lime over the top of the pile and cover that with a thickish layer of soil. The pile will now probably be about 1 ft. (30 cm) high.

3. Add some blood and bone meal or old, dried manure or some dried chicken pellets. Continue piling and adding manure every 1 ft. (30 cm) until you have a 3 ft. high pile. Leave it to decompose but keep an eye on it to see it doesn't get too wet or dry.

4. When the leaves are nicely rotted, break the pile down and give it a good chopping with a spade, or you could spread the layers out and run the lawn mower backwards and forwards over them a good few times. This will ensure there are no compacted lumps left. Running fingers through any compacted bits and pulling them apart can be quite pleasant.

Hydroponics

Hydroponics is another form of no-dig gardening. Plants are grown in a soil-less medium, such as expanded clay or gravel. They are bathed in or suspended over a solution of water and nutrients. Hydroponics is a great way of gardening for people who have problems bending over—the plants can be grown in benches raised to a convenient height.

is not constantly digging around their roots and damaging or cutting them off. Any weeds that do appear can be pulled out by hand.

A conventional vegetable garden can be turned into a no-dig garden by a mulch of straw, alfalfa hay, seaweed, or similar organic mulch between the rows so that the soil is covered to a depth of 3–4 inches (8–10cm). This will conserve moisture and suppress weed growth so that there is no need for any digging.

Companion Planting

Plant companions are those that help each other grow when planted together. The benefits can be varied and while the trial and error of generations of gardening passes on some of nature's secrets, others are yielding to scientific research. Consumer demand for environmentally friendly garden products is increasing interest in phytochemicals and their role in the garden.

Sometimes one plant will help another by attracting beneficial insects, such as bees that aid in pollination, or predatory insects that control pests. The pretty annuals *Nemophila* and poached egg flower, *Limnanthes*, for instance, attract predatory flies, while dill attracts the tiny wasps that like to feed on aphids. Other plants may repel pests through the aromatic oils in their leaves. This is the most common use of plants in 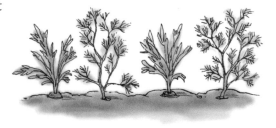 companion planting. Strong smelling herbs, such as tansy, marjoram, and sage, are planted through the garden to deter pests that don't like the smell, and to confuse other pests who find their way to food sources through smell.

 The exudations from the roots of some plants inhibit pests or diseases in the soil or, in other cases, assist growth by enriching the soil. The actual growth of plants can also have benefits.

Plants with deep or strong root systems

often have the ability to break up hard soils, or draw nutrients up from the subsoil. Others concentrate certain elements and when allowed to decompose on the garden bed, increase the supply of that nutrient to other plants.

Companion planting is recommended to the organic gardener as an important tool in establishing healthy, well-balanced growth. But the kinds of changes in health that companion planting brings about are not immediate. The gardener brought up on the almost instant gratification of technological fixes might be disappointed by the slow response, but once you adjust your internal clock back to the rhythms of nature, you'll appreciate the changes.

PLANT	LIKES	DISLIKES	EFFECTS
Basil	Tomatoes	Rue	Improves growth; intensifies flavor of tomatoes, repels flies and mosquitoes
Borage	Tomatoes		Deters tomato worm, strawberries, squash
Chamomile	Cabbages, Onions		Improves growth
Chives	Carrots, apples		Reduces risk of apple scab
Dill	Cabbage and other brassicas, corn	Carrots, tomatoes	Improves growth
Garlic	Raspberries, roses, fruit trees	Beans, peas	Improves health
Hyssop	Cabbage, grapes	Radishes	Deters cabbage moth
Marigold	Many plants		Discourages nematodes, bean beetles and other insects
Mint	Cabbage, tomatoes		Deters white cabbage moth
Nasturtium	Radish, cabbage, curcubits		Deters aphids

" The best fertilizer is the
gardener's shadow."

....

~Author Unknown

Chapter 3

Fertilizing the Garden

G rowing healthy plants requires a sensible feeding program. Most plants benefit from fertilizer dug into the soil before planting and followed up with regular applications thereafter. The environment benefits when those fertilizers come from natural sources. The range of organic fertilizers is large, and contains some sources you may not have considered. Choose from those described below, the fertilizers that are easiest for you to source, and that meet your garden requirements.

Animal Manures

Animal manures are rich in the

Mulching Tips

– A mulch should be between 2 to 4 inches thick for maximum benefits.

– Coarse mulch will stop weeds better, while a fine mulch will decompose easier, creating a need for more frequent mulching.

–Before mulching, remove weeds and soak the soil.

–Never mix mulch in with the soil, only place it on top.

– A thick layer of newspapers makes a good mulch, and since most inks are vegetable based, they are nontoxic.

–Don't let mulch touch the stems of your plants. Only much to the "drip line" outside of plants.

essential plant nutrients NPK (nitrogen, phosphorus, and potassium). Good garden manures include those from cows, horses, donkeys, sheep, pigs, and from more unusual sources such as camels (in some country areas), elephants (available when a circus is in your area), and ZooPoo, a mix of mainly herbivore manures from the zoo.

Poultry and pigeon manures are also useful. The availability of pigeon manure depends on knowing someone nearby who keeps pigeons, but poultry manure is easy to come by. It is sold commercially in pelleted form and is also available from roadside stalls in rural areas. The best poultry manure to buy this way is from poultry kept on deep litter that produces a well-composted strawy manure with more humus content than straight manure.

I have sometimes been able to obtain a load of strawy duck manure, which gives great results spread liberally over the whole garden. But a warning: duck manure needs to be well composted to reduce the smell.

Manure smells generally are not a problem, but sometimes the demand for natural products catches up with the supply and you can end up with a "fresher" product. If this happens and find you have spread a stinking mulch, don't panic. Hosing over the treated garden beds twice daily for a couple of days will help disperse the odor and wash the source of it down into the soil.

But don't overdo the watering; you don't want to lose the value of the manure in run-off. Avoid spreading manures on very hot days when the heat will generate stronger smells.

Stable manure is a "value-added" product as it is a mixture of horse manure and strawy stable sweepings that add extra humus. It is available either free or very cheaply from stables and riding schools. You usually have to provide your own bags or trailer and sometimes have to sweep it up yourself too.

Cow manure is generally sold at nurseries in bags as milled cow manure. This is safe to use and weed-free. Country gardeners will be able to gather their own manure from a local field. When gathering wild manure, cast your eye over the field and avoid collection from an area with obvious bad weeds; you could be letting yourself in for years of weeding.

The best place to locate sheep manure is under old shearing sheds where it has been composting down for years. Cultivate country friends with access to shearing sheds. When you visit, take a few large bags and a shovel in the trunk of the car. Even better, take your trailer.

Man Manure

Animal manure is fine, but the ultimate manure source is treated sewerage sludge. Sewerage sludge is an important source of manure, but is

making liquid manure

To make your own liquid manure all you need is a large container to hold water, a burlap sack, and some animal manure. Some plants, such as comfrey, can also be used. Most animal manures can be used, but sheep manure is particularly high in nutrients.

*You should water the soil before using your home-made liquid manure. To use a foliar spray the liquid should be diluted with equal parts of water.

1. Fill a drum with water and collect a bag of animal droppings. Tie some twine at the top to create a loop.

2. Put a piece of wood across the top of the container and suspend the bag in the water. Leave the bag for about 2 weeks. The water will go dark brown. Remove the bag and cover the drum.

often neglected.

Though there are various forms of composted sewage sludge available, the general public is generally squeamish about the idea of composted sewage sludge as garden manure. Certainly the organic gardener should be aware of this valuable product of recycling and make use of it in the same way as other animal waste products.

The sewage sludge is composted with wood waste for 12 weeks and reaches very high temperatures, which kill any

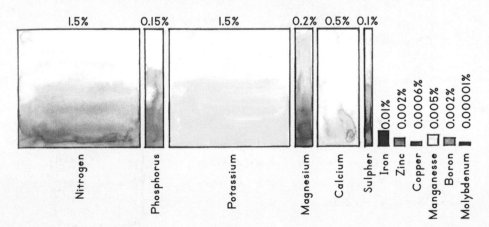

Elements Required for Healthy Plant Growth

Nitrogen	Phosphorus	Potassium	Magnesium	Calcium	Sulpher	Iron	Zinc	Copper	Manganesse	Boron	Molybdenum
1.5%	0.15%	1.5%	0.2%	0.5%	0.1%	0.01%	0.002%	0.0006%	0.005%	0.002%	0.00001%

potentially harmful organisms. The compost is also tested for the presence of heavy metals and is guaranteed safe for use.

Ocean Manure

The ocean provides us with wonderful organic fertilizers including fishmeal and seaweed. Seaweed has been sustaining agriculture in the sands of coastal areas and on barren islands off the coasts of Ireland and Scotland for centuries. It is a rich source of humus and minerals.

Gardeners living in areas where seaweed gathering is not an offense have a wonderful advantage. Seaweed can be used as a mulch directly onto the soil, without the need for washing or composting. If you have a heavy soil, you could compost the seaweed before using it. Pile it in a heap, water over it, and then cover with a layer of soil and a sheet of heavy-duty black plastic. This will keep the pile intact, keep the flies away, and help speed up the composting process.

For those with no access to free seaweed, seaweed products are available commercially in liquid form, Maxicrop, for example. These are valuable soil improvers, feeding the microorganisms in the soil, which have an important relationship with root growth.

Alternatively, you can buy bags of organic seaweed compost or decomposed mulch. The seaweed compost conditions garden soil by improving the mineral balance and can also reduce the need for watering. Seaweed mulch is claimed to give roses a boost, producing early budding and long-lasting and vividly colored flowers. Seaweed contains plenty of potash, which makes it particularly useful for mulching tomatoes, which have a high potash requirement. Use it around other fruiting and flowering plants for good results, too.

Waste products from fish processing are another excellent source of fertilizer. Fish products tend to smell fishy and this adds to their aura for some organic gardeners. This is the "If it smells bad it must be good" theory. The smell wears off quickly when commercial fish products are used

in the garden, but until it does, expect your cat to
take a keen interest.

A light watering will help disperse
the smell by washing residues off foliage
and helping the fertilizer to soak down
into the soil.

Fish is an excellent fertilizer, more
readily used in the home garden when
packaged. Don't be tempted to dig leftover fishy bits into your
garden because all the local cats and dogs will converge to dig
them up. You can also find fish conveniently packaged in liquid.
It is excellent to water on to growing vegetables and annuals and
outdoor pot plants. But don't use fish emulsion on indoor plants
because the fishy smell will not appeal to anyone but the cat
who may damage the plants in an effort to find the source of that
alluring scent.

Other Organic Fertilizers

Apart from manure, there are several
other forms of organic fertilizer,
including blood and bone, bone meal, and
dried blood. These are also available in liquid
form, such as Nitrosol. Blood and bone
is a great standby for the green gardener

and it is frequently recommended as a good organic plant food, but there are vegetarians who are not so keen. While I don't think plants and pets should be obliged to be vegetarian along with their owners, I do concede that handling blood and bone would be a real turn-off for the dedicated vegetarian. The good news is that there are substitutes that can be used to give a similar effect. Blood and bone is a slow release fertilizer that contains nitrogen and phosphorus, both of which can be obtained from other sources. The usual animal manures contain nitrogen and phosphorus as well as potash (NPK), the big three life-giving soil elements.

Earthworms concentrate phosphorus (plus many other good things) in the soil and can be encouraged by the use of plenty of mulch and compost. Worm casts, the complete and perfect plant food, are available by the bag from nurseries or can be produced in a personal worm farm.

There are many sources of nitrogen. All liquid fertilizers, for instance, are high in nitrogen. Nitrogen can also be added to the soil by growing nitrogen-fixing crops of legumes (peas, beans, lupins, clover, and alfalfa) as green manure that is dug in.

"No occupation is so delightful to me
as the culture of the earth, no culture
comparable to that of the garden . . .
But though an old man, I am but a
young gardener."

....

~Thomas Jefferson, *Garden Book*, 1811

Chapter 4

Mulch

A mulch provides great labor-saving benefits for the green gardener. It slows down the evaporation of moisture from the soil, lowering watering requirements; it insulates the roots of plants from excesses of temperature; it slowly breaks down to add nutrients to the soil; and it helps stifle weed growth. A mulch can be either organic or inorganic (obviously only organic mulches break down to aid soil structure and nutrient content), simply consisting of anything that will blanket the surface of the soil. The best mulch for your garden will depend on what you have access to and the special conditions of your environment.

Proceeds from Processing

Food processing plants are a wonderful source of organic compost. For instance, firms that make instant coffee have large quantities of coffee grounds; wine makers have grape marc (the seeds and skins left after pressing); sugar mills produce bagasse; pea growers have pea straw; peanut factories have nut shells; rice mills have vast quantities of rice hulls; apricot canners have apricot kernels and so on.

One of the most exciting forms of mulch I have ever encountered is cocoa waste. Besides smelling great, cocoa waste composts down well and its color blends with the soil and plants.

Grape marc is much in evidence on gardens in wine-growing areas and can be used as a mulch to keep weeds down. It also makes an excellent surface for paths.

Rice hulls are available from rice mills, and they will probably give them to you by the trailer-load, though bags are also commercially available. Rice hulls can be dug into heavy soils and will be a help for new gardeners wanting to improve the drainage of heavy clay soils. They can also be used as a mulch, but tend to blow about in windy weather.

Where they are available locally and are either free or very cheap, I would recommend their use to start a new garden where they can be dug into the soil. However, once the garden is established, other mulching materials will be found more effective.

Lucerne Hay

A bale of alfalfa hay is a wonderful

asset to the garden. Spoiled alfalfa hay that cannot be used as feed is great for the garden. Alfalfa hay can be spread thickly over garden beds, between rows of vegetables, and as a mulch around newly planted or established trees and

Why Mulch Your Garden?

Apply to your vegetable garden in the second week of spring each year:
1. Imitates the nutrient-saving nature of the forests.
2. Eliminates water splash and the soil-borne diseases.
3. Suppresses weeds.
4. Controls nutrient loss through leaching in heavy rain.
5. Prevents the soil getting a hard crust.
6. Encourages wormlife to work at the soil's surface, accelerating soil improvement.
7. Adds humus, adding organic matter to the top of the soil.

shrubs. It suppresses weeds, keeps the soil from drying out, and composts down to enrich the soil.

Spread and watered over with seaweed extract you will get the same benefits as using seaweed without the need for a trip to the beach. If alfalfa hay is not available, use straw.

Country gardeners will have ready access to hay (especially old hay) and town gardeners can  buy bales at produce stores. One of the advantages of alfalfa hay is that it is usually reasonably weed-free. Alfalfa is a legume crop and fixes nitrogen for its own use. This means that the plant has a high nitrogen content and, when used as a mulch, the nutrient becomes available to the plants in a slow-release protein form.

Alfalfa is recommended to rose growers because of its slow-release nitrogen and good potassium levels, the essential nutrient for flower production.

Other advantages of a mulch of alfalfa around roses (and other plants) is that the light color reflects heat in summer months and keeps soil

cooler. A cover of alfalfa suppresses weeds and conserves moisture. Alfalfa also stimulates root growth, apparently due to natural hormones in the hay, and encourages earthworm activity. And there's more: research has found that root diseases are suppressed in soils mulched with alfalfa.

Some rose growers also claim that they have less trouble with black spot—the fungal disease that is often a problem for coastal gardeners—when they use an alfalfa mulch.

Spread alfalfa hay in spring and again in mid-summer, in a layer about 2 inches (5cm) thick. Water it over when bud development starts with liquid seaweed fertilizer for a good flower flush. Alfalfa can be used with a complete plant food with an NPK level of around 10.3.15.

Leaf Mulch

Leaf mulch from deciduous trees in the garden is the crop your garden produces and should be returned to the soil to enrich and protect it. Rake leaves off lawns and paths and put directly around shrubs and trees. In cold climates, a mulch of leaves right over cold-tender perennials such as cannas will protect them. Surplus leaves can be put into the compost heap or bagged and left to break down slowly.

Lawn Clippings

Never use fresh lawn clippings directly on the garden—they will heat up and rot any plant that comes in contact with them. However, if you need a quick supply of mulch, lawn clippings can be spread out and left to dry for a week or so. They can then be raked up and used by sprinkling thinly around plants as a light mulch.

A safer use for lawn clippings is in the compost. Lawn clippings heat up really well in a compost heap and compost down rapidly if mixed with other materials—straw, manure, vegetable peelings, light prunings, and leaves—which keep the grass aerated and stop it from matting.

If you have too many lawn clippings for the compost bin, put them in a separate heap and each time you mow the lawn give the heap a fork through, then add the new layer and top it with a couple of spadefuls of soil, manure, or organic fertilizer. Keep covered with a sheet of heavy-duty plastic. You will find the grass will compost down rapidly through the warmth of summer. In spring it will be ready to use and you can start a new heap when the mowing season starts again.

Weeds

Weeds can be used by the organic gardener, either in the compost or as mulch. It is important not to use weeds with seeds, but annual weeds cut or pulled before they set seed can be used. If perennial weeds are used, it is important to remove bulbous rootstocks as well as seed heads to avoid creating a worse weed problem.

Using a mulcher

A mulcher is the best help the home composter can have. All garden clippings, prunings, even moderately sized branches can go through the mulcher for instant mulch, which can be added to the compost heap or used on the garden. You'll never need to put garden prunings in the garbage again. The only problems are that mulchers are expensive and take up a lot of room in the garden shed. Get around these drawbacks by sharing the cost with a couple of neighbors. Alternatively, pile up your heavy prunings in some out of the way place until you have enough to put through a hired mulcher in half a day. That way you don't have to worry about maintenance or storage.

Newspaper

Newspapers can be shredded or laid flat, well overlapped, to a depth of ½ inch (1cm) to suppress weeds and retain moisture. Always water the soil before laying a mulch of newspaper and do not let it come in contact with the stems or trunks of plants. Newspaper is a wood product and as such is

fully organic and will compost down into the soil. The thicker the layer of paper, the longer it will take to compost down, but don't expect it to return to the soil in anything under three months.

Newspaper mulches need to be covered to prevent them from blowing about. The print on newspapers does not cause any problem as modern methods of printing do not involve lead or any other contaminants.

Sawdust

Hardwood sawdust can be used as a mulch and can be added to compost. Sawdust is best piled up, hosed over, and allowed to weather before it's put on garden beds. When using it in compost, sprinkle it in a thin layer, one or two spadefuls at a time, so that it is distributed evenly through the other compost materials.

Pine sawdust will produce a very acidic compost and if you want to use this it will be necessary to add lime to the heap to counteract the acidity. Before using compost that contains a lot of pine sawdust, check the pH with a soil testing kit. If it is acidic, add a dressing of lime, moisten, and fork over and then leave for a couple of weeks and test again

before using. Of course, acid-loving plants such as azaleas, camellias, and rhododendrons will appreciate a compost that is on the acidic side.

Do not add the powder from floor sanding to the compost heap; it is so fine that it simply clogs up and becomes an impenetrable mass. If an old floor is being re-sanded, it will contain waxes, varnish, paint, or other surfacing materials previously used on the floor, which won't be good for the garden.

An excellent way of using large quantities of sawdust if you have a ready and cheap supply is as a thick mulch on paths, particularly between vegetable beds. After it has been used on the path for a few months, it can be turned into the soil and a fresh layer put down on the path.

Many commercial potting mixes contain composted sawdust pine bark. Most orchid mixes, for instance, contain various grades of pine bark to give an open mixture.

Pine Needles

Pine needles and needles from other conifers form a mat under the trees. This is best left in place as it is the natural way for the trees to grow and the mulch provides a weed-free environment under the trees. If the mulch becomes too thick, it can be raked up and composted, It is best distributed through other compost materials with the addition of lime and manure.

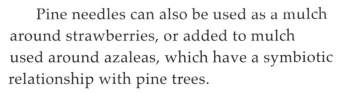

Pine needles can also be used as a mulch around strawberries, or added to mulch used around azaleas, which have a symbiotic relationship with pine trees.

Bark Mulch

Bark mulch has been popular with what I think of as non-gardeners for years. Pine bark provides a neat, tidy cover that suppresses weeds and does not decompose readily, which is of course the main attraction.

But because it does not break down readily, it does not add

any nourishment to the soil in the way that other organic mulches do. For this reason, I do not recommend the use of pine bark to mulch native plants. Native plants have a symbiotic relationship with microorganisms in the soil that helps root growth. A mulch which does not compost down to provide food to sustain these microorganisms will result in starved and weak plants.

Pine bark chips are available in several grades from coarse to fine. Pine flake is also available which provides an attractive mulch for paths or can be used as a ground cover for areas of the garden not suitable for lawn or as a deep mulch in a children's play area. Pine bark products come from pine forests planted for harvest and use parts of the trees once regarded as waste. In this respect they are biologically sound. Some pine forests, however, have been planted on what was once native forest, felled for the purpose of replanting with pine trees; hardly a green practice.

Inorganic Mulch

Gravel, pebbles, and crushed rock can all be used as a mulch and work well in suppressing weeds, keeping the soil moist and cool and providing a good environment for earthworms. They do not, of course, add extra humus to the soil, which is one of the big benefits of using organic mulch.

A gravel mulch works at keeping the soil cool and retaining moisture because it heats up during the day when the sun shines on it. The warmth draws water up from the soil, but it condenses under the rock or stone and, when this cools at night, the moisture drips back into the soil.

In areas of high wildfire danger, a pebble mulch of some kind is much safer to use than any organic mulch that will add to the fuel supply for a wildfire. Pebble mulches are also valuable in inland areas where materials for surface mulches are scarce.

For gardeners who use pebble mulches but worry about the need to get more organic material into the soil, wait for a rainy period when there is very low wildfire danger. Rake the pebbles back and add a good mulch of compostable material

mixed with manure. Water well, then spread the pebbles back into position.

The mulch should compost down within three or four months so that by the time the wildfire season comes around again it won't be a problem.

Weed mat is another inorganic mulch, a wonderful product that is an updated and much more environmentally sound version of the dreaded black plastic that so many gardens were smothered by in the '60s and '70s. In fact, weed mat does all the things that people expected, in vain, of black plastic.

Weed mat suppresses weeds effectively because it excludes light so that weeds are unable to germinate. It does not break up with exposure to sunlight and is long-lasting. It is kind to the soil as the fine mesh lets oxygen and water into the ground. Aeration of the soil means that vital microorganisms can continue to flourish. Allowing water in supplies roots already established in the soil. Soil covered by weed mat stays sweet and healthy, unlike soil covered by the old black plastic which became evil-smelling.

New plantings can be made to weed-matted areas by cutting cross-wise slits, folding back the cut edges and planting through the hole. Don't attempt to plant weedy weed-matted areas for at least several months, though, to give the weeds time to die off. If you have an area of intransigent weeds that colonize strips of garden along fences or under trees, spread weed mat over the problem area and leave permanently in position. Cut down taller weeds before spreading the  mat. Weeds with dense growths would need to be raked hard to allow the mat to be laid. Smaller weed growths can simply be covered. Excluding the light will stop the covered plants from growing—they can't get through the tiny holes in the mesh and there is no need to use any herbicides. The mat can be covered with mulch to improve its appearance.

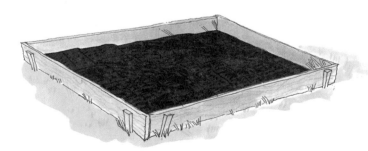

Black plastic sheeting should never be used in the garden as a ground cover; it damages the soil and breaks down in sunlight. However, it is useful in the vegetable garden where strips are used under strawberries, lettuce, and some other crops to suppress weeds and reduce watering. At the end of the season, the plastic strips are removed and discarded.

"And so it criticized each flower,
This supercilious seed; Until
it woke one summer hour, And
found itself a weed."

....

~Mildred Howells

Chapter 5

Saving Water

Any home gardeners are anxious about the rising cost of water and fear that "only the rich will be able to have a garden." In fact, it is very easy to grow a garden that does not need vast quantities of water. Many plants are drought-tolerant once they are established and even lawns are becoming more environmentally sound as drought-tolerant grasses are developed.

In fact, most gardeners

waste water. Consider how often we walk down the street and see water running down a driveway and into the gutter from a sprinkler left running on a lawn. How often do people waste water by hosing down paths and nature strips to clear away leaves and rubbish instead of using a broom? Or use the hose to wash the car when they could do the job better with a bucket or two of water?

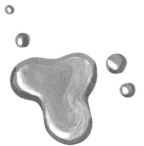

And how many gardeners waste water through incorrect watering techniques. A quick sprinkle is the worst. It merely wets the soil surface where it quickly evaporates. Frequently wetting the soil surface encourages roots to stay near the surface looking for water where they are quickly burned off when the soil dries out. Deep watering once or twice (in summer) a week will ensure that the water soaks down to the roots.

Some gardeners are also responsible for water-wastage through run-off. They have paved so much of the garden that rain-water runs off into storm-water drains instead of soaking down to replenish the water-table. In some suburbs where there

a lot of tennis courts and other large paved areas in home gardens, this run-off actually causes local flooding. And the moral from that story is: concreting your garden over does not save water. On the contrary, it wastes it.

Saving the Bath Water

Household town water can be recycled by using the bathwater for the garden. The easiest way to do this is to put a length of hose into the bath and siphon the water out of the window. Have someone holding the other end of the hose do the watering. We did this for years when we were on a pump-out septic tank system and, with a family of four children, found that if we let

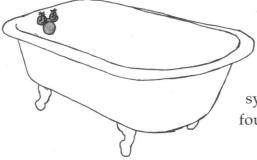

Fill Up the Tank

One of the most effective ways for the home gardener to save water is to install a tank to collect run-off from the roof. Suburban gardeners will find that especially designed small tanks that do not take up a lot of space or intrude on garden design.

Large tanks can be installed out of sight under houses that are built on sloping ground or on high stumps. If you are planning a new house and hope to have a garden, it is worthwhile investigating the possibilities of installing an underground tank to provide water for garden use. In country areas or areas of wildfire danger, a tank of rainwater will provide a back-up water supply that can be used in an emergency.

Just as installing a solar energy hot water system may not deliver an immediate saving, providing a large water tank is a long-term cost reduction measure. And the real point is not so much your individual finances, but the resource bottom-line of the whole community. As well as using less water and so reducing the need for more dams to be built, you'll also be doing your bit to reduce run-off from roof guttering that helps flood storm-water drains and pollute rivers, streams, and harbors.

the bathwater and washing water go into it, the tank overflowed, causing a big problem.

The garden being established on the bathroom side of the house was watered totally with bathwater with great success and much saving in the cost of extra tanker services to empty the overflowing septic tank. A brick in each of the flush cisterns also helped to reduce the water use. Half-flush systems can be bought these days if you are installing new toilets and want to stop water wastage.

Using washing water on the garden can have problems. Many washing powders contain boron, which can build up in the soil and cause boron toxicity. The best thing to use in your washing water is a soap-based product that does not contain boron. Add a water softener such as Calgon to the water to give you a good wash. When you use your soapy water, plants get more than simply the benefit of water. A half gallon (2L) of soapy wash water with the addition of a tablespoon of white oil is useful to spray over plants to control insect pests such as scale.

If you do need to use a washing powder or liquid, choose one that contains the lowest amount of boron (read the ingredients on the side of the package). Then again, you can avoid the boron

problem altogether by only using the rinse cycle for the garden. If you do use washing water on the garden, try to give an occasional deep watering with rain water or town water to help wash the accumulation of salts down into the soil away from the feeding roots. An application of gypsum every three to six months will also help.

Good Watering Techniques

1. Don't give gardens frequent light sprinkles. The water stays on the soil surface and quickly evaporates. Instead, deep water once a week (twice in hot, dry weather).
2. Annuals or newly-established plants should be given extra watering until they develop a deep and well-established root system.
3. Keep the garden well-mulched to reduce evaporation. Mulch needs to be a few inches (several centimeters) deep to do this effectively. Mulch when the soil is wet from rain or watering so that you know there is moisture there to retain.
4. Though some people believe a watering system wastes water and insist on hand-held hoses, a watering system that delivers a drip or spray of water directly to the root area of plants is a much more efficient way of watering than spraying a hose around.
5. A timer increases water efficiency.

6. Even without a full watering system, you can use water efficiently by putting a timer onto your tap and using a soaker hose that can be placed between the rows in a vegetable garden or through a garden bed to deliver a measured amount of water to the root area without any waste.

7. The best time to water is in the early morning. This gives the soil plenty of time to warm up and the plant foliage time to dry off. Plant roots are not very active in cold, wet soil, so plants will grow better when the soil is warm and moist through the day. Watering in the evening leaves foliage wet overnight and this increases the likelihood of fungal diseases developing in the moist, humid conditions.

8. There are, however, several advantages to only being able to water in the evening. It is very relaxing and cooling to stand out in the garden in the dusk listening to the gentle sound of the falling water as you wave the hose about after a hot summer day. Cooling the garden will also make the house more pleasant as cooled, sweet air drifts indoors. Watering at night also ensures that the water will not evaporate quickly and the soil will stay damp overnight and early morning.

Watering Established Trees

If you have established trees and shrubs in the garden, they will be fairly self-supporting, but will need some watering in hot, dry periods. Watering over the soil surface is not very effective—often the water doesn't penetrate far enough through the soil to reach the roots. A more efficient, water-saving method is to place a length of terracotta agricultural pipe down into the soil under the canopy. Water directly into the pipe. A large tree will need two or three pipes placed at intervals around it. A shrub may need only one. Citrus trees can be watered very efficiently this way in times of drought and water shortage.

Where water is almost always in short supply, put the pipes in when you plant a tree or shrub and make a practice of watering into the pipes.

The water will soak down better if you water a surfactant into the pipes every three to six months. This will make the soil more water absorbent. A handful of complete fertilizer can also be dropped into the pipes every three to four months to get nutrients down to the roots.

Choose Drought-tolerant Plants

Growing drought-resistant plants is a sure way to cut down on the amount of water needed in the garden. Many people believe that this means that they can only grow native plants. However, there are many other plants that can be grown to beautify the garden that do not require frequent watering. Plants with succulent stems or leaves, including members of the succulent and cactus family are adapted to withstand long dry periods and make good potted or garden plants that won't require much watering.

Perennial plants with a permanent bulbous or thickened root stock do not need constant watering, though they will flower better if they are given some watering at flowering time and flowers will last longer if they are given a drink while in bloom. Some suggestions for flowering plants that seldom require additional watering once established are listed below.

Agapanthus

Evergreen clump plants for a sunny position. Glossy green, fire-resistant foliage and blue or white heads of lilies in summer.

Clivia

Evergreen clump plants suitable for filtered sun or part-shade with heads of salmon to scarlet flowers in winter/spring.

Dietes

Taller sword-like, evergreen clumps of foliage with iris-like blooms (white with mauve markings or yellow with brown splash) periodically through much of the year. Suits full sun to filtered or part-sun.

Gazania

Ground-covering daisy plants that thrive in sandy soils and full sun. Many-colored daisies bloom right through warm weather.

Geranium

Botanically Pelargoniums, these plants survive
well on little water and flower freely in a range
of bright colors in a sunny spot.

Duranta

Tall-growing shrub
suitable for hedges, long
season of blue flowers
followed by yellow berries.

Oleander

Wonderful shade-giving,
drought-tolerant flowering
shrub that will thrive inland or
by the sea. Flowers from spring to autumn in
white, pink, salmon, and crimson. Suitable for
high hedges, privacy, or can be grown as a small
tree.

Plumbago

Shrub with light green
leaves and masses of blue
or white summer flowers. Suitable
for hedges, around swimming pools,
and over fences.

Carob Bean

Ceratonia siliqua is a useful shade and fodder tree, good on farms. The fruit, the carob bean or St. John's bread, is a nutritious chocolate substitute and stock feed.

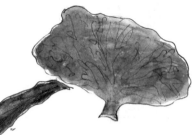

Desert Ash

Fraxinus oxycarpa is a boon to dry areas. A deciduous tree, up to 40 feet (12m) in some conditions, but smaller on poor dry soils.

Peppercorn Tree

Schinus areira syn *molle*. Graceful shade tree with evergreen, lacy, weeping foliage widely grown in country areas for its shade and drought tolerance.

Planting for Success with Minimum Water

Remember that all plants must become established before they are able to survive drought, so careful planting and some aftercare is vital for success.

1. Make plantings at the time of the year when rain is expected in your area. This should ensure some water to help get plants going. Autumn or spring plantings are best in most climates. Avoid planting in summer when more watering will be needed for survival.

2. Planting out from small tube-stock will give better results than planting large, container-grown trees, as the young, developing root system is better able to establish itself.

3. When doing mass plantings over large areas, have the soil tilled first. In a new home, garden rotary-hoeing is a good way of opening up heavy soils.

4. Treat heavy clay soils with gypsum before planting. This can be broadcast over tilled or rotary-hoed areas or, in the garden, added to individual planting holes.

5. Never plant into a dry hole. Have a bucket of water beside you and a ladle. Pour some water in and wait for it to soak away. Your plant won't be as likely to suffer from transplant shock if the roots go into damp soil.

6. If the water in the hole doesn't soak away within a minute or so, you will need to improve the drainage by adding gypsum.

7. Use water crystals. Water crystals swell and absorb water providing a reservoir of moisture that is available to plant roots for quite a long period. They will reabsorb water from subsequent watering or rain. Water crystals go into the bottom of your planting hole, can be covered by a thin layer of soil, and water added so that they swell. The tree is then planted as usual.

8. Water again after planting and mulch (with straw, hay, or grass and weeds cut from the planting site).

9. In cold districts, a planting bag will protect young trees. Push three or four stakes in around the plant. Pull a plastic bag over the stakes. Plastic tree bags can be bought or you can recycle plastic bags from the supermarket by opening the bottom.

10. If mulch is scarce, place a large flat stone or several large pebbles beside your tree. The hot sun will draw up the water, which will condense under the stone and fall back into the soil.

11. Give follow-up watering after a week or ten days if no rain falls.

12. Trees from autumn plantings can be given a dressing of complete fertilizer or Osmocote or Nutricote in spring. Native trees need not be fertilized, but if fertilizer is used it should be either something organic like blood and bone, or

something formulated specifically for native plants.

13. Don't plant more trees in one year than you can spare the water for. You will have a more successful result if you get one batch of trees well-established, then concentrate on a second planting the following autumn when the first lot are self-supporting.

"Show me your garden and I shall tell

you what you are."

....

~Alfred Austin

Chapter 6

Wildlife in the Garden

Birds

The green gardener can have fun matching wits with garden pests. One battle that is never-ending is the contest between the birds and the gardener. Gardeners spend half their time encouraging birds to visit the garden to help control pests and the other half trying to keep them away. Birds that eat fruit, vegetables, newly planted seeds, and seedlings are not welcome.

There are many safe ways to keep them at

bay. If you have fruit trees or berry fruit, the best way to save the fruit from the birds is to net the trees or berries. Many commercial orchards are now completely netted and growers are amazed at how much extra fruit they harvest once the fruit bats and birds can't get access to it.

Netting over trees must be firm so that the birds don't get trapped in it. The easiest way to ensure this is to put up a light frame right over the tree and cover it firmly with bird netting. This can be taken down and stored after harvesting.

Berry fruit that grows on a trellis, such as raspberries, can be netted in a similar way. Strawberries can be covered with portable chicken wire frames.

Fear is an age-old technique for keeping the birds away and birds are just as scared of snakes as most humans. It is easy to fool the birds with a rubber snake (buy them at joke shops or at National Parks Shops). Put the snakes out in the garden, in trees, or where needed, and move them about from time to time so that the birds don't get accustomed to seeing them in the one spot. My favorite snake "scarecrow" is jointed and sways about most realistically. Don't leave your snakes lying about when they are not actually needed. familiarity breeds contempt.

Gardeners have also tried scaring off birds with humming lines, flashing silver foil, milk bottle tops strung on strings criss-crossed across vegetable beds, cardboard cut-outs of hawks dangling above the beds, or the old-time scarecrow. To have any effect, this last suggestion needs lots of fluttering, glittering bits and pieces hung from it. An artistically picturesque scarecrow will look pretty in a cottage garden, but won't scare away too many birds.

Bird damage might also be averted by spraying with quassia spray. It is very bitter tasting and simply puts the marauders off your harvest. Quassia spray (made from boiling quassia chips up into a "tea") washes off as soon as it rains or even after a heavy dew and must be constantly renewed to have any effect.

Some gardeners try to avoid damage to clusters of fruit, such as figs, by tying them in mesh bags like the ones in which you buy oranges.

This has some deterrent effect if you can keep the mesh away from contact with the fruit, so that the birds can't peck it through the mesh.

Commercial banana-growers cover their bunches of ripening bananas with specially made, open-ended plastic covers (blue, yellow, or orange) to protect them from fruit bats and birds. Birds are generally only a problem when bananas begin to ripen so that if you pick the bunch as soon as the first banana begins to ripen and hang it up in the garage, laundry, or any airy, convenient place indoors, you can beat the birds. But fruit bats seem to visit frequently to check out the bunches and the developing fruit becomes covered in scratches, damaging it even before they get to eat it.

If you can spare the water in dry times, occasionally direct the hose over a patch of well-mulched ground just next to your garden. A damp leaf mulch will help maintain the insect population. This will give the birds a scratching alternative to your garden.

Encouraging native birds by planting

bird-attracting flowers is good insect control. But don't make the mistake of putting out food to attract large numbers of birds. When you tire of putting out the free food, they'll become a problem. If you must put out food, put out a certain amount and don't increase it in response to increasing numbers at the same time each day. And remove it after a time, about an hour.

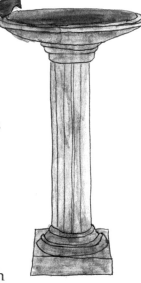

Canned pet food is recommended for meat-eating birds, birdseed for seed-eaters and, for honey-eaters, properly balanced bird nectars are available from pet shops. Don't put out honey as this can lead to diseases among honeybees.

A clean source of water in the garden is important for birds, especially in dry weather. A birdbath should be high enough to protect the birds from cats and close to tree branches or shrubs that will provide shelter. Change the water daily so that it doesn't become disease-laden or a home for breeding mosquitoes.

Other Visitors

Lizards of all kinds are garden friends because they live on insects. They won't hurt humans, but are themselves in danger from our pets.

Some lizards, such as geckos, live in the house and feed on insects at night. Others, such as blue tongue lizards and water dragons are great at cleaning up snails in the garden. If you are fortunate enough to have blue tongues or water dragons, don't use snail bait around the garden as the lizards may eat the poisoned snails and be poisoned in turn.

A few chickens in the back garden are great for providing fowl manure, eating insects, and supplying fresh eggs. Half a dozen fowls on deep litter will provide great mulch and they can be let out to free-range in sections of the garden for a few hours each day. A portable wire-mesh frame is needed for this. You must put your chickens safely in their fowl house at dusk to protect them from foxes and dogs.

Ducks are great for eating snails, but one or two are

enough—more will turn your garden into a duckyard—in other words, bare dirt.

Geese are great only if you have plenty of space, such as a grassy field (with a pond or dam) where they can be fenced off from house and garden. They make good watchdogs and keep down grass and weeds, but are not suitable for the average suburban garden.

"We have descended into the
garden and caught three hundred
slugs. How I love the mixture of
the beautiful and the squalid in
gardening. It makes it so lifelike."

....

~Evelyn Underhill, *Letters*

Chapter 7

Controlling Pests and Diseases

Being a green gardener is not an excuse for allowing pests and diseases to ravage your plants undeterred. Instead, the green gardener applies treatments that will control pests in a way that is not harmful to the environment. This may involve picking pests off by hand or using natural controls, some of which are available commercially, others are homemade.

Companion planting is another natural method of controlling pests and so is being aware of natural pest controllers, such as ladybugs and predatory mites. Planting

French lavender
will grow in most
soils and is good
for dry corners, hot
spots, near walls
or next to paths
for its fragrance,
which is released
as passersby brush
past it. The plants
may need trimming
to prevent them
sprawling or
becoming woody as
they mature.

bird-attracting plants helps maintain the balance of insects in the garden. And using good planting techniques, such as crop rotation and companion planting, reduces the build up of pests and diseases.

But don't expect the organic garden to be pest-free. To maintain the population of predatory mites and other insects and birds, you need a few insects for them to eat. Otherwise they'll die out or move to another garden. The aim is a natural, healthy balance.

If you find that a plant is constantly attacked by pests or disease, it means that it is unsuited to the situation (the wrong soil, wrong climate, or not enough sun, for example) and is weak. A plant that can't grow in your garden without frequent spraying has no place in an organic garden. Concentrate instead on what can be grown easily.

Weak plants actually attract insect

pests that can smell the difference between a healthy and an ailing plant. Strong plants are full of chemicals and resins that actively deter pests. In fact, serious insect attack is often the first sign of a sick plant.

But insects don't just appreciate sick plants; they also like to feed on soft new growth. Everyone who has ever had a garden will have noticed that as soon as new, tender growth starts in spring, the population of sucking and chewing insects explodes to take advantage of the feast.

The most noticeable insect attack in the garden is probably the aphids, which cluster thickly on new rose shoots. They multiply at a bewildering rate because in spring the aphids are almost all females that produce live young without the need to spend time mating and laying eggs.

As soon as you see the aphid populations building up in spring, you must take steps to control them. This is important because these insects spread viruses and virus-like diseases.

Neglect early in the season brings more problems later in the year. Aphids can be controlled by rubbing them off with the fingers (wear a rubber glove for this), brushing with a small paintbrush, or hosing. This will have to be done each day and is usually only practical if you have a very small garden. Nor is it much help waiting for the natural predators to clean them up for you. The ladybugs, lacewings, and hoverflies are great helpers, but don't breed in enough numbers to make much impression until summer.

For good control of aphids and other pests, you need to start in winter. Winter spraying with Bordeaux and white oil will clean up over-wintering pests, eggs, and fungal spores. But don't spray these together; leave at least a week between separate sprayings. As soon as they appear in spring, aphids and other sucking insects can be sprayed with non-toxic commercial sprays such as soap sprays and pyrethrum sprays;

or homemade insect sprays concocted from garden plants such as rhubarb leaves, elder leaves, tomato leaves, or wormwood.

A tablespoon of pure grated soap can be boiled up in a quart (1L) of water and added to any of these leaf-tea sprays to help them stick. A tablespoon of white oil can also be added to sprays to help them stick and to add a smothering effect to the toxic effects of the actual spray. Fewer insect pests will be attracted to the garden if you don't overdo the fertilizer, particularly nitrogen fertilizers that encourage a lot of new, soft growth. It's satisfying to see plants putting on that juicy, lush spring growth, but if you can think of it as laying on a spread for an insect feast, you may choose a slower, steadier growth rate.

Using mulch, compost, and manures will ensure steady, healthy but not over-lush growth on plants. Remember, however, that sometimes lush growth is necessary. Vegetables grown for  a leaf crop, such as lettuce, for instance, will need suitable feeding to encourage quick, tender growth.

Growing a good mixture of different plants is another way of ensuring that you don't get a big build up of one particular pest. This is an extension of the practice of crop rotation. For instance, if you only grow a few roses, you may not have any trouble with black spot and other rose pests and diseases. Once you have beds filled with them, though, the populations build up to take advantage of the supply.

One of the simplest ways of avoiding the use of chemicals or sprays of any kind is to grow resistant plants wherever possible. When buying seed, read the label and when possible grow a variety that is resistant to some diseases.

Cucurbits (any gourd plant: cucumbers, pumpkins, zucchini, etc.) are prone to powdery mildew. All apple cucumbers are, for instance. But some cucumber varieties, such as Green Gem, are resistant.

Fusarium Wilt attacks cucurbits and tomatoes. Again there are some resistant varieties including the Burnley Gem tomato.

Many heritage vegetables are resistant to fungal diseases, which is why they have survived in home gardens for so long. Check seed catalogs for heirloom varieties.

Even given all these good garden practices, there may still be times when you do need to use a chemical spray. Fruit fly, for example, is a serious pest of orchards that you are obliged to control with chemicals. Use a recommended spray in an emergency and in association with all your usual green methods.

Correct and efficient spraying ensures that the weed is

killed before it can set seed, preventing serious infestation the following year. Small, spot infestations can be weeded or dabbed with sulfate of ammonia.

Don't despair if you do occasionally have to use chemical cures. Follow the directions on the pack carefully, be cautious, and wear protective clothing. A combination of good housekeeping (cleaning up debris, rubbish, weeds, and culling sick plants) in the garden, crop rotation, a variety of plant materials, insect traps, and regular use of organic sprays will make sure that resorting to harmful chemicals is a rare occurrence.

Attracting the Right Insects

An interesting aspect of environmental pest control is to grow plants that will supply food for predators of common insect pests. These plants will re-seed and become a regular part of the garden, encouraging beneficial insects and birds to colonize your garden and help you avoid the use of chemical sprays.

You will need an area of about 22 square

feet (2 square meters) or more to create a low maintenance block of carefully selected flowers and grasses that provide a beneficial insect habitat. Providing food and shelter will attract friendly insects. But sometimes waiting for a healthy natural balance to assert itself isn't good enough. Large scale gardeners buy in the mercenaries, predatory insects bred as pest control armies. Mealy bug, for instance, is difficult to get rid of and is a common pest of greenhouses.

For the green gardener, it's a case of know your insect. The ones pictured on the following pages are all worth cultivating in your garden.

Mealy Bug

Good Bugs

Dragonfly

The nymph lives in water and feeds on mosquito larvae. The nymphs also provide food for fish. Adult dragonflies, graceful, gauzy creatures, catch mosquitoes and midges on the wing and are an ornament to any green garden.

Assassin Bug

Both nymph and adult bugs feed on other insects. The sharp proboscis can pierce the hardest shell and suck the juice from the victim's body.

Bee

One of the most useful of garden insects, bees are important pollinators (both honey bees and native bees) and their presence is essential to ensure a good crop on many fruiting trees and vegetables.

Green Lacewing

A night-flying insect with gauzy wings and large eyes that you will sometimes find coming in the windows at night. The larvae, which are called "ant lions," feed on insect pests. They are raised commercially and are used as important biological controls of major insect pests. The brown lacewing has larvae so hungry they are known as "aphid wolves"—good insects to have in the garden.

Ladybugs

Most gardeners know that the ladybug, a pretty red, yellow, or orange spotted insect, is a friend. Ladybugs feed on aphids, mealy bugs, white flies, scales, and the eggs of other insects. The larvae can eat up to 50 or 60 aphids a day. Ladybugs will not feed on insects being tended and protected by ants, so control ants if they are running about among shrubs, trees, and other plants that are infested with scales, mealy bugs, and aphids.

Praying Mantis

These are quite large green insects that are often mistaken for grasshoppers or stick insects. They fold their front claws as if in prayer and snatch up any insect that comes near. If you see these delicate green mantids in your garden, don't damage them, they have a big appetite for pests.

Frog

Frogs and toads are useful residents in the garden as they have big appetites for all kinds of insects.

Parasitic Insects

These are valuable controllers of pest populations as they lay their eggs in the bodies of adults, larvae, pupa, or eggs of the host insect. When the parasitic egg hatches, the larvae feed on the body of the host and destroy it. Ichneumon wasp larvae feed on caterpillars and grubs that damage food crops. The adult has a long, thin body with long, thread-like antennae. Trichogramma wasps are too tiny to be visible. They move through the garden laying eggs within the eggs of other insects—over 200 insect pests are hosts of this wasp, including leaf-cutting caterpillars.

nets to catch night-flying insects in late summer and autumn. These are "good guys," not to be thoughtlessly squashed. In spite of the fear many gardeners have of spiders, most of them are beneficial garden inhabitants.

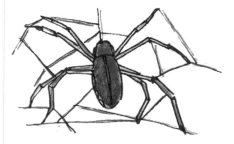

Wasps

Most gardeners fear wasps, but the native wasps (such as the paper wasp that lives in paper-like nests hanging from branches and eaves) feed on insects and are valuable predators, hunting

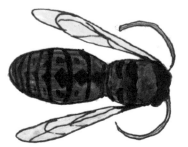

Spiders

These are important predators feeding on many insect pests. Orb-weaver spiders put up huge

caterpillars such as corn ear worms, armyworms, and cabbage worms to feed their young. But these are not to be confused with the European wasp, which is a dangerous pest. Its nests are usually found in the ground, banks, foundations, tree stumps, and similar places. Call a pest control company if you find one of these.

Ground Beetles

Larvae and adults eat caterpillars, armyworms, cutworms, maggots, and others.

They may be black, brown, or brightly iridescent.

Hover Flies

Hover flies get their name because of their habit of hovering motionless in the air. The adults feed on nectar and pollen but the larvae feed on aphids.

Robber Flies

Robber flies catch insects on the wing or crawling on the ground, spearing them with their sharp proboscis. In the larval stage they live in the soil where they feed on other insect larvae.

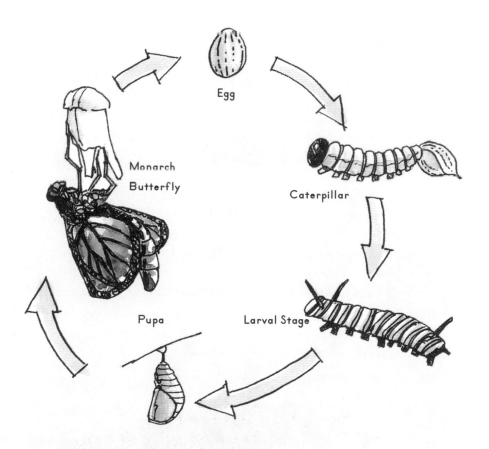

Egg

Caterpillar

Monarch Butterfly

Larval Stage

Pupa

Know Your Caterpillar

In late summer and autumn the large citrus butterfly is a beautiful visitor to the garden. The caterpillars feed in citrus trees and also in some natives that belong to the same family Rutaceae. The caterpillars are green, brown, and white and resemble bird droppings. Usually there are not many of these in a citrus tree and there is no need to kill them. If there are large numbers, squash some but leave a few to grow and turn into beautiful butterflies.

One caterpillar every gardener should be able to recognize is the caterpillar of the white cabbage butterfly, which is smooth and bright green. Don't spare this pest or it will chew vegetables belonging to the cabbage family, including stocks and wallflowers.

Some caterpillars feed on weeds, so they could be described as friendly—the main food of the larvae of a brown butterfly is a weed of lawns, cudweed. The Wanderer or Monarch butterfly larvae feeds on milkweed, also known as swan plant.

Some gardeners plant the butterfly shrub, *Buddleia*, to attract butterflies to the garden. This is a popular food plant for a number of butterfly larvae so, if you grow *Buddleia* for the butterflies, be prepared to put up with some chewed leaves.

Sprays for Pests and Diseases

These days you don't have to go into witch's mode over a steaming cauldron in the kitchen to use natural sprays. Because of the increasing demand for "safe" sprays, many are now available commercially.

Available sprays include: pyrethrum sprays, eucalyptus spray, garlic spray, soap spray, white oil, *Bacillus thuringiensis* (Dipel), sulfur dust, Bordeaux, lime sulfur, copper oxychloride, potassium permanganate (Condy's crystals), rotenone dust or sprays (Derris Dust), and Safer.

Synthetic hormone control is an important control for pests. Check for new developments in this field. Most householders are aware of sprays that control pests, such as fleas and cockroaches, by preventing breeding through the use of synthetic hormones. Many lures use sex pheromones to trap insects with the idea of breaking the breeding cycle.

Homemade sprays using ingredients from the garden are easily made and environmentally safe as they have a short life. This means they won't contaminate the soil or poison birds or lizards. It also means they must be used more frequently than most commercial sprays that have a longer life.

Of course environmentally safe doesn't mean non-toxic and some of the homemade sprays are poisonous. Rhubarb and nicotine sprays, for instance, are particularly dangerous if ingested.

Most homemade treatments are best used quickly rather than being stored, as they lose their effectiveness over time.

Recipes

Basic Soap Spray

This can be used against many insect pests on its own or can be added to other homemade sprays to help them stick.

Recipe: 1 tablespoon pure soap flakes or grated soap. Pour over enough boiling water to dissolve well. Dilute with 2 quarts (2L) of water and spray when needed.

Notes: This spray can be made more effective by adding 1 tablespoon of white oil to the mixture. It will be even more effective with a "knob" of washing soda added and dissolved in the boiling water. The stronger spray is very useful for scales and can be sprayed or brushed on.

Bordeaux

This is a good fungicidal and bacterial spray that can be bought commercially. But the homemade version is fresher and more effective.

Recipe: Mix 3 ounces (90g) blue copper sulfate and 7 quarts (6.5L) water in a plastic bucket. Stir well to dissolve. In a second plastic bucket mix 4.4 ounces (125g) calcium hydroxide (hydrated lime), if

possible from a freshly opened bag, in 2.5 quarts (2.5L) water. Mix the two liquids together, stirring well. Use immediately.

Notes: Bordeaux is best used in winter on dormant plants at bud swell. It is toxic to fish and overuse may kill earthworms. Wear gloves when handling Bordeaux.

Bug Juice Spray

This effective spray is for the green gardener with a strong stomach.

Recipe: Gather about half a cup's worth of whatever pest is the problem in your garden. Put them into an empty jam jar with a screw top lid so they won't escape. Pour a little hot water over them to kill them. Put the bugs in a blender with about two cups of warm water and blend to a soup. Pour into a glass jar and leave the bug puree on a warm windowsill. The next day strain, then dilute the remaining liquid with water at the rate of 1 part juice to 50 parts water. Spray immediately over plants needing protection.

Notes: If you use caterpillars for this spray, you are, in effect, making a spray similar to *Bacillus thuringiensis* (Dipel). This commercial spray is based on a bacterium commonly found in the gut of caterpillars that turn into moths or butterflies. Other insects may find the smell of the bug spray threatening, though it may also contain natural pathogens that will kill the insects.

Bugbane

Gardeners can now grow this shrub, *Cimifuga racemosa*, from seed. Follow the sowing directions on the packet carefully.

Recipe: When the plant has grown, gather a handful of leaves, chop, cover with boiling water, and leave to stand overnight. Strain and spray at the rate of 1 part bugbane to 4 parts water.

Notes: Bugbane leaves can also be dried and used in sachets among clothes or in drawers and cupboards.

Balm of Gilead

The camphor-scented leaves of balm of Gilead, *Cedronella triphylla*, repel insects. Green gardeners grow this in the garden among plants to repel insects and also rub leaves on skin when gardening to keep off mosquitoes and flies.

Cedronella triphylla

Chamomile tea

Sprayed frequently on fruit, chamomile tea will protect against brown rot, and when sprayed around seedlings, offers protection against damping-off.

Recipe: Make up a normal pot of tea, using a tea bag, which is easier than searching for enough chamomile flowers. Cool before using.

Notes: Chamomile is a useful activator in the compost heap.

Chamomile

Chinaberry Spray

Chinaberry *Melia azederach* is an attractive garden tree. Gather half a bucket full of leaves and berries; cover with boiling water; cool and strain. Spray all pests including snails. Another species of *Melia*, native to India and other parts of Asia, known as the Neem tree is a widely used traditional insecticide and is even better than the chinaberry if you can get it. The leaves can be dried and powdered and used as a dust or spray. Dried leaves can be used in cupboards to repel insect pests.

Clay

Here's an old-fashioned treatment for scale.

Recipe: Mix some heavy clay (fine potter's clay would be suitable) with enough water to make a sprayable mixture. Strain if grainy or it will clog your sprayer. Mixed to a thicker consistency, it can be painted on stems with a brush.

Dipel

A biologically sound control based on *Bacillus thuringiensis.* Make your own by blending or mashing a cup of caterpillars and 3 cups just warm milk.

Leave for three days in a warm place, then strain. Dilute at the rate of 1 cup mix to 8 cups water and spray.

Elder

This is a good general spray against pests and can also be used as a fungicide.

Recipe: Put 1 pound (500g) leaves and stems of the attractive shrub elder, *Sambucus nigra*, in a large pot and cover with 3.5 quarts (3.5L) of water. Bring to a boil and let simmer for 30 minutes adding more water if necessary. Cool, strain, and spray.

Notes: This spray will keep but is poisonous and should be labeled and kept out of the reach of children.

Elder

Eucalyptus

This environmentally sound treatment can be bought commercially, which is the easiest option. It is best used in cool weather as spraying on hot days can cause leaf burn. Use it to control scale and other sucking insects.

Lime

Here's an unusual treatment to clean up snails in clump plants. First hose plants, such as clivia and other clumps, which are prone to heavy snail infestation, making sure to wet under the leaves. Then, dip a soft woolly cloth into lime, hold it well into plant and shake vigorously. Lime will fly up and cling to the wet leaves.

Notes: Don't use this treatment around azaleas, camellias, and other acid-preferring plants.

Marigold Aphid Spray

Recipe: Pick a handful or two of marigold flowers, some stems and leaves (the stronger smelling the better) and cover with boiling water. Let stand overnight, then strain and add the liquid to soap spray.

Nicotine

An effective, if poisonous, insect spray can be

made from tobacco leaf plants.

Recipe: Boil leaves in water, cool, strain, and spray. If leaves aren't available in your garden, boil up a packet of cigarettes in a large saucepan of water (use an old saucepan for this). Allow to cool then strain and spray. Make and use as needed.

Notes: Don't spray tomatoes with nicotine and do not smoke when gardening near tomatoes, as this can spread viruses and disease. Keep nicotine spray away from children.

Potassium Permanganate

Recipe: Add a few grains of potassium permanganate (Condy's crystals) to a bucket of water enough to color it pale pink. Use as a fungicidal spray.

Pyrethrum

A shop is the easiest place to obtain a pyrethrum spray, unless you have space to grow a good supply of pyrethrum daisy, *Chrysanthemum cinerarifolium*. It is an attractive plant with silver-gray foliage and white daisy flowers.

There are also many safe and effective sprays manufactured from

synthesized pyrethrum (permethrin) that work the same way as natural pyrethrum but are effective for a little longer than the 24–48-hour life of pyrethrum. Use it as a general insecticide for aphids, thrips, whitefly, two-spotted mite, azalea lace bug, etc.

Recipe: If you grow pyrethrum daisy, soak 2 tablespoons of dried flowers in 2 quarts (2L) of hot soapy water. Stand overnight, strain, and spray insect pests.

Chrysanthemum cinerarifolium.

Notes: Plant pyrethrum daisy among vegetables such as members of the cabbage family as a companion plant to repel pests.

Rhubarb

Rhubarb leaves are poisonous and can be used to make a bug "tea" for sucking and chewing insects.

Recipe: Simmer about 2 pounds (1kg) of leaves in 3 quarts (3L) of water for 30 minutes. Add a tablespoon of soap flakes, cool and strain. Bottle and label clearly "poison."

Notes: Keep rhubarb spray out of the reach of children.

Rotenone Dust or Spray (Derris Dust)

Rotenone (Derris Dust) is effective against sucking and chewing insects including caterpillars, pear and cherry slugs, and aphids, but use it with care if you have an ornamental pond or a dam as it will kill fish and frogs. Rotenone breaks down after a few days in the sun so dust frequently over cabbages and other leafy plants.

Rue

An attractive garden shrub with ferny, blue-green foliage, rue, *Ruta graveo,* lens is a good deterrent for dogs and cats. Plant rue where dogs create a problem or sprinkle freshly chopped leaves over a newly dug and planted area to deter animals from digging among new plantings.

Sacred Basil

Easily grown through the warm months, sacred basil has a much stronger aroma than other basil species. The fresh leaves can be rubbed on exposed skin areas to repel mosquitoes when gardening and they also make a useful insecticide.

Rue

Recipe: Put a good handful or two of leaves into a plastic bucket, crush, then cover well with boiling water. Leave to steep until the "tea" is dark brown. Strain and spray sucking and chewing insects.

Salt

Common salt is a poison and should be used with restraint. It can be used as a weed killer if spread over weeds in paths on a hot day or works as a snail killer when hand picked snails are dropped into a bucket containing hot, salted water.

Seaweed

Gather seaweed, rinse if salty, then put into a plastic bucket or drum, cover with water and leave for a few weeks until water is brown. Use as a fungal and bacterial spray. Spray at any time even on a regular weekly basis as it is an excellent fertilizer and soil improver.

Stinging Nettle

Though not very person-friendly, stinging nettles are an important part of the green garden. They are a compost activator and foliar fertilizer and can also be sprayed to control aphids.

Make a "tea" by covering nettles with boiling water. Let steep until a good color. Strain and dilute to weak tea color with water and spray liberally and often.

Stinging Nettle

Sugar

Sugar and molasses can both be used as

a soil drench to kill nematodes. Dissolve 4½ pounds (2kg) in a bucket of water.

Sulfur

Powdered sulfur (flowers of sulfur) can be used to control mites. For mite control, water plants to be treated making sure leaves are wet underneath. Put sulfur powder into an old nylon stocking or muslin bag; hold hand well into plant and shake vigorously. Dust will fly up and cling to undersides of damp leaves. Use in the cool of the day to avoid burning. Buy from a drugstore or hardware store.

Tomato Leaf Spray

Take a handful of tomato leaves, put into a plastic bucket, and cover with boiling water. Cool and use as a general insect spray. Repels flies and aphids. This is poisonous and should be used at once and not stored.

Urine

This is the ultimate "do-it-yourself" spray and a very old home gardener's fungicide, traditionally used for apple scab, among other things. Use fresh, diluted in a bucket of water. Spray mildew and other fungal diseases on plants.

It will also act as a liquid fertilizer. Use fresh and do not store.

White Oil

Many gardeners get carried away with using white oil, which is seen as a very "safe" spray, and use it indiscriminately. It is a useful winter spray for dormant plants and is a good treatment for some insect pests including scale, but is not suitable for treating fungal diseases.

Like soap, it is a useful additive to organic homemade plant or herb sprays. Do not use it undiluted. The usual rate for use is 1 part to 20 parts of water. Spray in the cool of the day.

Tip: Don't use white oil sprays during hot weather as they cause leaf damage when the temperature is over 75°F (24°C).

Wormwood

Wormwood *Artemesia spp.* is a popular garden shrub grown for its silvery-gray foliage and an old-time insect repellent (fleas, moths, and other pests). A species grown in China has been used for centuries to treat malaria. Wormwood tea can be used as a general garden insecticide. Use leaves and flowers, gather a convenient quantity, chop and put into a plastic bucket. Cover

with boiling water and let cool and stand for several hours. Strain and use diluted at the rate of 1 part wormwood tea to 4 parts water. Can be watered around the dog's kennel and put in the rinse water when pet's bedding is washed. Also used as a bath rinse to repel fleas.

Trap that Pest

While most gardeners have been conditioned by commerce to think of sprays first when a pest becomes a problem in the garden, traps can be very useful control methods. Traps should join sprays as part of the green gardener's armory.

Fly traps

These are simple, very effective methods of trapping fruit fly, blowflies, and other insects. Fly traps are not effective on their own in eliminating fruit fly.

Some fruit fly traps are available commercially. You can also make your own fruit fly traps easily and cheaply. Cut the top off an empty soft-drink bottle to form a funnel. Make a hole in the side of a second bottle and push the "funnel" in at an angle. The angle should prevent rain running in. Mix up a teaspoonful of honey and ripe banana pieces and enough water to make it a pouring consistency. Pour about an inch (2–3cm) into the bottle. Screw the cap on and hang the trap in a tree. The sweeter and more fermented it becomes, the more it attracts the flies. They enter the trap through the funnel shape in the side but cannot escape as they fly up towards bright light to find the exit. The funnel-shaped side entrance obscures this.

Alternate ingredients can be other sweet and yeasty things, such as orange peel or bran. To attract moths, such as the codling moths hanging around the apple trees, try wine and a little water in the trap.

These traps also work near the barbecue, around horse yards where flies worry horses and near the dog kennel if outdoor dogs are troubled by flies. In areas where blowflies are really bad, some people use a bit of liver and water in the trap—smelly old liver will certainly draw the blowflies, but hang it well out of nose reach if you want to enjoy your barbecue. Inspect the trap or traps in your trees and when you see fruit flies being caught, use splash baits on foliage, branches, trunks, and any nearby fence, but of course not on the fruit itself.

All Fired Up

Maidenhair ferns often become infested with pests like mealy bug and scale. The easiest way to deal with this is to cut the fern back. Make a spill of twisted paper, light it, and set fire to the fern stalks. Do this in a safe place. The stalks will blaze up for a few seconds and all pests should be destroyed. Then water and cover your fern with a plastic bag, held away from the plant by a hoop of coat hanger wire pushed into the pot and fastened with string or an elastic band to form a mini greenhouse. Place pot in a cool, sheltered spot and in a couple of weeks fresh, healthy new fronds will shoot up.

Snail traps

There are many snail traps and most green
gardeners will have a favorite—my favorite is
the pet food trap. Snails and slugs are drawn
irresistibly to canned pet food. They also like
to congregate in damp, cool, dark places. This
trap provides both to make a snail heaven.

Take a length of terracotta agricultural pipe and dampen it well.
Lay it in the garden next to your vulnerable seedlings, bulbs, or
vegetables. Place a spoonful of pet food in the middle (cats and dogs
won't be able to reach it). Every morning check your pipe and scrape
the congregated snails into a bucket containing some hot salty water.
This will kill them instantly. Re-bait the trap. Check daily.

Snails that have climbed up into trees (citrus and tree tomato
are favorites) or tall-growing plants such as dahlias will not be
attracted down to the ground by baits. Instead, try spraying the

trunks and stems (and under the leaves in the case of
dahlias) with Bordeaux or wormwood spray.

An excellent system of snail control, if you can
spare the time, is to go out into the garden on damp,
cool evenings with a flashlight and a bucket of salty
water and prowl around your garden. Pick off the
snails and drop them into the bucket. This can be
quite an exciting occupation for the green gardener

made desperate by the depredations of the little devils.

Other traps include beer traps. Place beer in a container and sink it into the soil so that snails attracted to the beer can reach it easily, fall in, and drown. Even easier, leave beer cans with about a teaspoonful of beer still left in them lying on their sides in the garden, and collect and dispose of daily. Half orange skins and hollowed out potato skins will also attract snails, while rings of dry sawdust or ash around plants will protect them from snails as the snails can't slide over these surfaces. Containers with turn-over edges are snail traps in themselves, as gardeners with potted plants will know. Run a stick under the edge regularly to rid yourself of unwanted visitors.

Slater traps

Hollow out potatoes and place near infestations of wireworms and slaters. They will move into the potato. Empty potato traps daily into a container with a little water and kerosene.

Wrap traps

Many pests call be trapped by wrapping trunks in materials such as burlap or corrugated cardboard. Caterpillars, such as the codling moth, can be trapped by tying overlapped material around a tree trunk.

Some moth caterpillars crawl down the trunk looking for a sheltered place to rest during the day and hide in the folds of the bagging or cardboard. Daily inspection and removal of clustered caterpillars will control this pest very easily. Cardboard can be burned complete with caterpillars or shaken into a bucket with a little kerosene and water; material can be scraped to remove caterpillars (kill as above) and re-used. Wrapping can be completely removed when two or three weeks of inspection yields no more pests. Codling moth caterpillars crawl down the trunk to pupate in loose bark, rubbish, or old fruit boxes. Remove loose bark and clean up any trash and timber lying about under trees. Wrap trunks in corrugated cardboard or something like an old wool sweater. Check at least once a week and destroy any trapped pupae. Adult codling moth is active from late winter through spring with peak activity in April/June.

The moth is about an inch (22mm) across and gray-brown with a dark, shiny area near the wing tip.

Put up bands as soon as you see a codling moth in your lure (wine and water trap hung in apple and pear trees) or at petal fall and use until after apples have been picked.

Note: Trapping only stops the next generation—it won't protect the apples already on your tree. It is important to use trapping as an adjunct to spraying with *Bacillus thuringiensis* (Dipel) when adult moths are around.

Earwig traps

Place rolled up newspapers or corrugated cardboard beside plants being attacked by earwigs and check each day for earwigs that crawl in to rest.

Earwig traps can also be made by first pushing stakes into the soil beside infested plants. Then push an empty can or plastic flower pot stuffed with crumpled paper onto the stake. Remove and burn paper or drop it into bucket of soapy water. Cardboard rolls from plastic wrap can be pushed upright into soil beside infested plants instead. Save halved orange skins after juicing, place cut-side down—earwigs will

move under to shelter.

Grease Bands

These can be used to control pests, such as fruit tree weevil (and also ants which farm aphids and scale) that crawl down the trunks of plants to pupate in the ground. The adult crawls back up the trunk to breed and start the cycle again. Make sure no branches touch the ground and put grease bands on the branches and trunk.

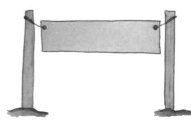

Painted Boards

Whitefly builds up in numbers periodically and becomes a serious pest of plants like tomatoes, beans, other vegetables, and passion fruit. Trap boards are very effective in controlling them (and other pests like aphids) along with pyrethrum or other organic sprays.

You will need several boards about 12 inches (30cm) wide painted bright yellow (use enamel paint). Coat boards liberally with a clear grease. Hang on stakes between plants, on the fence, and around the vegetable garden. When coated with insects, wipe clean and reapply grease. (Grease must be clear so as not to obscure the bright yellow color).

Shiny Foil Sheets

Insect pests flying about in search of food or host material to lay eggs need to know which way is up—the brightly lit sky is up. If you spread reflective material such as strips of aluminum foil roofing insulation (use off-cuts) between the rows in the vegetable garden, pests, such as cabbage white butterfly for instance, are dazzled by the reflected "sky," become confused about where to land, and fly away. Combine this with confusing smells by interplanting vegetables with strong smelling plants like marigolds, sage, and other herbs.

Going Organic

PEST	PROBLEM	CHEMICAL	GO GREEN
African lawn beetle	Curl grubs eat roots in lawns and gardens.	In spring apply Nemacur and water well.	Dig over garden beds to expose larvae so birds can eat them. Water lawn with Baythroid in spring when larvae is close to the surface
Ants	Ants are mostly a problem when they nest in pots or garden plants.	Treat nests and trails with diazinon.	Ants like dry nest sites so keep pots well watered and add moisture-holding compost and water crystals; stand pots on bricks painted with kerosene.
Aphids	These tiny insects multiply rapidly on new growth. They spread virus and disease and damage shoots and buds.	Spray with malathion.	Rub off with fingers or a good strong jet from the hose; spray with pyrethrum or soap sprays.
Azelea lace bug	This is a tiny bug that feeds on the underside of leaves.	Spray with dimethoate.	Spray under leaves with homemade nicotine spray mixed with a tablespoon of white oil.

PEST	PROBLEM	CHEMICAL	GO GREEN
Bean fly	The larvae tunnel into stems and leaves and weaken plants that fall over or break.	Spray with dimethoate.	Apply rotenone dust or spray (Derris Dust) every three days. Hill up soil around base of plant to encourage new roots to help support plants.
Caterpillars	These voracious feeders attack vegetables, fruit, foliage, and flowers.	Spray with malathion.	Spray with *Bacillus thuringiensis* (Dipel).
Cutworms	The grubs live in soil and begin feeding at the base of plants, later moving upwards.	Spray with carbaryl.	In the evening, scratch soil around base of plants that are vulnerable to attack, such as seedlings and beans, and powder well with ratenone (Derris Dust). Rotenone can also be used on the foliage and *Bacillus thuringiensis* (Dipel) can be used as cutworms become moths.

PEST	PROBLEM	CHEMICAL	GO GREEN
Citrus Leafminer	Plant leaves become curled and distorted with wavy white lines running through them. The larvae tunnel through leaves and pupate in curled leaf edges. The cycle takes three weeks.	Spray with malathion or dimethoate.	Spray frequently with pyrethrum when the tiny, silvery-white moths are noticed.
Codling Moth	The grubs feed in apples and pears.	Treat with diazinon at petal fall. Carbaryl can be used after 30 days from full bloom.	Bag tree trunks with burlap or corrugated cardboard. Inspect for pupa and destroy frequently. Spray with *Bacillus thuringiensis* (Dipel) when moths appear in lures. Remove fallen fruit, flaking bark and broken branches, old timber, etc.

PEST	PROBLEM	CHEMICAL	GO GREEN
Cottony Cushion Scale	Scale is covered with a white wax.	Spray with malathion.	Spray with white oil in late summer to early autumn; ladybugs are often predators of this scale.
Earwigs	They are brown to black insects with a pair of pincers at back.	Spray with carbaryl.	Traps made with rolled newspaper or crumpled paper pushed into pots will trap insects. Gather and drop into soapy water.
Fruit Fly	The grubs in fruit cause rotting.	Spray with dimethoate.	Remove and destroy rotten and fallen fruit. Use lures to trap flies and begin treatment when numbers build up.
Lawn Armyworm	The caterpillars feed on lawns and do severe damage.	Spray with carbaryl.	Water lawn at dusk with *Bacillus thuringiensis* (Dipel). Moths seen around lights in the evening are a clue to check the lawn for damage.

PEST	PROBLEM	CHEMICAL	GO GREEN
Scale	Scale may be white, pink, brown, or black and it covers the underside of leaves along the veins. It may be accompanied by ants or sooty mold.	Spray malathion and white oil.	Spray with soap spray and white oil.
Mealybug	The oval insects are fringed and covered in white wax. They attack ferns and indoor plants, succulents, etc.	Apply disyston granules to soil.	Spray with white oil diluted 1 to 20 with water.
Two-spotted Mite	These tiny mites feed under leaves, causing graying of foliage on beans, azaleas, and others.	Spray with dimethoate.	Water under foliage and then shake flowers of sulfur into plant so that the fine dust sticks to the underside of leaves.

PEST	PROBLEM	CHEMICAL	GO GREEN
Tomato Russet Mite	Mites can be seen with a hand lens under leaves and on stems. The lower leaves are attacked, becoming brown and papery. Pests move up stems and eventually attack flowers and fruit on tomatoes, peppers, eggplant, and potatoes.	Spray with dimethoate or malathion.	Use sulfur dust or wettable sulfur, but not in hot weather.
Whitefly	These tiny white moth-like insects fly up when disturbed and attack beans, tomatoes, etc.	Spray with dimethoate or malathion.	Paint 12-inch (30cm) square boards bright yellow and cover with clear grease. Place around plants to trap whitefly. Spray with pyrethrum as well if infestation is heavy.